The American Century Series

MADISON
CONNECTICUT
IN THE TWENTIETH CENTURY

Charlotte L. Evarts and Sidney L. Evarts were citizens of 20th-century Madison whose roots reach back to the the town's earliest days. Their love of life and concern for their community were an example to their family, friends, and all who knew them. This book is dedicated to their memory.

THE AMERICAN CENTURY SERIES

MADISON
CONNECTICUT
IN THE TWENTIETH CENTURY

Warner P. Lord and Beverly J. Montgomery

ARCADIA

Copyright © 1998 by Warner P. Lord and Beverly J. Montgomery.
ISBN 0-7524-0940-9

Published by Arcadia Publishing,
an imprint of Tempus Publishing, Inc.
2 Cumberland Street
Charleston, SC 29401

Printed in Great Britain.

Library of Congress Catalog Card Number: 98-86604

For all general information contact Arcadia Publishing at:
Telephone 843-853-2070
Fax 843-853-0044
E-Mail arcadia@charleston.net

For customer service and orders:
Toll-Free 1-888-313-BOOK

Visit us on the internet at http://www.arcadiaimages.com

CONTENTS

The steeple of the First Congregational Church of Madison is a familiar local landmark.

FOREWORD

The seed that has grown into this book was planted by Nikki Gallagher in the fall of 1997. During a visit to the Charlotte L. Evarts Memorial Archives to research the history of political parties in Madison, she commented that an interesting fund-raising project might be to write a pictorial history of Madison in the 20th century.

The Archives Board asked the Madison Historical Society to participate in the project, Bev Montgomery agreed to be co-author, and the book began to take shape. Arcadia Publishing Company was contacted, and a representative came to Madison to discuss the proposal. In June 1997 a formal contract was signed.

As Bev was busy with other projects, I began the process of outlining the book, contacting resource people, and searching for photographs. The thought of finding approximately two hundred suitable photographs at first seemed daunting. I thought we would have great difficulty finding images for the 50s, 60s, and 70s, but my fears certainly did not materialize. It was soon apparent that the problem was not finding photographs, but deciding which ones not to use!

To understand the important changes in Madison during this century, I first read through all available town meeting minutes and Annual Town Reports from 1900 to the present. I recorded dates, grand list totals, school population figures, and significant actions taken by selectmen and town meetings. The data was entered into a computer database and sorted by date. This produced a time line of significant events in Madison's history from 1900 to the present.

The second task was to study the maps stored in the town clerk's office to find subdivision maps. Another database was created from these property records. This done I began to outline the significant events of each decade. I printed lists of photographs available at the Evarts Archives and matched these with the list of events.

Next I visited the Madison Historical Society to examine their collection. With Claire McKillip's help I found such treasures as Jay Clarks's series of photographs of commercial establishments in Madison in 1942 and an album of Horace Hunter's photographs.

By September 1997 much of the information had been gathered, but I wanted to be able to "see" the book as it took shape. I again turned to the computer and with a desktop publishing program created an exact representation of the book using the publisher's specifications for page size, type face, and image size. This allowed me to visualize the placement of the various images and better understand their relationship.

As the work progressed various themes began to emerge. It was readily apparent that Madison had changed significantly following the completion of the Connecticut Turnpike. The development along the shoreline that had marked the first 50 years of the century now spread inland to the rest of Madison. From 1,500 residents in 1900 the town grew to be a suburban community of over 16,000.

There was slow progression from a rural economy to one based on seasonal residents and then to that of a largely residential community. In the 1960s the Madison of the 1990s was born.

Bev Montgomery and I met in the fall of 1997 to coordinate our efforts. I had done most of the work up through 1960 and she agreed to work on the 70s, 80s, and 90s. Her task was a bit different as she often had to take the photographs that would illustrate Madison in the 1990s. In many cases she was able to contact the individuals and businesses that influenced Madison's growth during the final three decades of the century.

As the project progressed, we were privileged to see hundreds of photographs for the first time. In many cases we were allowed to make copies for use in the book. The task of preparing this book would have perhaps been impossible were it not for the many people who shared unique photographs, special documents, and wonderful stories of the "good old days."

Al Miller first introduced us to "Hilda's Diner" and shared first-hand stories of the 1938 hurricane. Whenever a photograph was needed, Al would find it. Sherry Clark of the George C. Field Company brought us family albums and Field Company records. Patricia Holdridge freely lent her collection of photographs of the Future Farmers Fair—none of which we had seen before. Mr. and Mrs. Stuart Hotchkiss provided the amazing picture of the upside-down cottage taken after the 1938 hurricane. George Gould seemed to appear weekly at the Archives with some new photograph or bit of information.

The *Shore Line Times* provided several photographs, including one of the dedication of the Scranton parking lot in 1952. The back issues of the *Shore Line Times* stored at the Evarts Archives proved invaluable in determining the precise dates of events. From the Connecticut Department of Transportation we acquired 80 photographs documenting the construction of the Connecticut Turnpike.

The book is the product of many hands. To each of you who had a story to tell, a document to share, a photograph to show—our sincerest thanks. We came to the end of the project with more information and photographs than we could possibly use. We are sorry if we left out something that you felt was important, but 128 pages fill rapidly. Perhaps we will publish a second volume!

The book is a gift to the citizens of Madison in the hope that they will develop a deeper appreciation for this unique and wonderful town. Read it, enjoy it—and continue to be a part of Madison's history.

Warner Lord
Madison, Connecticut
May 31, 1998

CHALLENGES AND CHANGES
Summer Colony to Sophisticated Suburb

Madison is a beloved town full of contrasts. A broad sweep of rocky headland and wave-washed beach are matched by the ancient rocks that tumble Ninevah's hemlock dark waters to the north. Boggy Coan Pond harbors cranberries in their season while from Buck Hill's lofty height, the Sound glistens in the sun. At rushing Iron Stream artifacts of ancient industries lie silently close by the handsome new houses on Race Hill Road.

On Main Street there is a constant bustle of business. Matronly Scranton Library surveys the scene as shoppers pursue their quests.

At the shore, rock-bound Tuxis Island lies quietly amid the rolling waters of the Sound while her namesake pond mirrors the ever-changing downtown scene.

From Summer Hill to Huzzle Guzzle, from Cole's Farm Stand to Stop and Shop, from the venerable Grave House to the condominiums nestled beside Hummers Pond—she is a place of contrasts, our beloved town—our Madison.

In 1650, Nicholas Munger established a homestead on the Neck River. He was the first settler in the area of Guilford that was to become East Guilford. The lands beyond the East River were the frontier of this new settlement. The early colonists were encouraged to settle these lands and establish homesteads.

By 1707, the East Guilford farmers had become so numerous they were granted permission to build their own church, and Rev. Jonathan Hart, the first graduate of Yale University, came to minister to them. The settlement continued to grow, and in 1826 the residents successfully petitioned the State of Connecticut for permission to become a separate town. By 1900, Madison was a town of 1,600 souls with a proud heritage in shipbuilding, commerce, and agriculture.

As the 20th century dawned, there was a fine new Memorial Hall, a library, a growing school system including Hand Academy, and an active citizenry. The first of many subdivision maps had been filed. Madison residents were beginning to sense they had something unique—open land near the sea and lovely beaches. Just the place for city dwellers seeking respite from their cares. When Mrs. Dexter of Detroit built the first summer house on Middle Beach in 1867, the locals thought her balmy. They could not know that their "worthless waterfront" would become a Mecca for city-bound seekers of sun and solitude.

J. Myron Hull, real estate and land developer, wrote in 1904 that Madison was: "an ideal place to spend the hot months, a town that is worthy of the attention of every person contemplating spending the summer away from the heat of the city or inland town."

The summer resident and the tourist soon captured the interest of local property owners. Chicken coops were transformed into tourist cabins and the farmlands of Middle Beach, Seaview, Buffalo Bay, and Webster Point became magnets for those with money to afford a summer home.

For decades, the streams and hills to the north of the railroad tracks lay largely untouched while the shoreline echoed with the sound of hammer and saw. But on January 2, 1958, the character of Madison was changed irrevocably. The Connecticut Turnpike opened. A great swath of newly laid concrete swept from east to west across the town underlain by the remains of homes and farms.

By century's end, the population had increased tenfold from 1,600 to 16,000; from two schools in 1921 to six in 1998; from a school population of two hundred in 1900 to more than three thousand, one hundred years later.

The journey through the century was alternately quiet and tumultuous. Flurries of change followed periods of calm. A citizenry of farmers and fishermen content with their town gave way to men and women of the world who sought a lifestyle better than that their parents had known. The years brought the modern conveniences of electricity, indoor plumbing, the trolley, the automobile, the airplane, the telephone, radio, television, and the computer. Madison today retains echoes of its past as a seaside town reliant on agriculture and a burgeoning tourist industry. The commercial district, centered around the Boston Post Road-Wall Street area, is quite different from the elm-shaded group of small stores which clustered there in 1900. The coming of I-95 removed the glut of truck traffic from Main Street and allowed the tourist and commercial traveler to speed past the town. The collective sigh of relief breathed when the turnpike opened was short-lived, however, and the desire to bring the traveler back to town was rekindled. On the eve of the millennium, Madison once more seeks to expand its offerings to the world.

The Chamber of Commerce in its 1997 brochure, Main Street and More, seeks to lure the wily tourist with these words: "Welcome to Madison—our historic, shoreline community with its wonderful mix of distinctive shops, charming restaurants, cafes and inns. You will find antiques, art, books, crafts, fashion, food and wine, gifts, jewelry, Main Street and more."

During the 20th century, the character of Madison was reshaped by economic, social, and political forces. Whereas the newcomer once sought a few weeks of relief from his urban cares, he now seeks a safe, small-town setting in which to raise a family. Madison has shed its rural skin and metamorphosed into a sophisticated suburban community, but those moving here are still drawn by its village charm, fine old houses, and rich New England heritage.

As ever, the past is tucked away in the woods and fields. Amid the developments, there are pockets of solitude and memory. The Genessee Colony in North Madison bears testimony to the hardiness of the early settlers who desired land to settle and to raise families and crops. Remnants of abandoned charcoal pits recall long-vanished industries. On the banks of the Hammonassett River, the trout fisherman casts his line in the shadow of a decaying mill dam. Gaunt pilings protrude from the East River recalling the Shoreline Electric Railway. From an abandoned cellar hole on Neck Road to the lovely old homes along the Post Road we are surrounded by the keepsakes of our heritage.

In 1957, the Shore Line Times noted that the buildable land south of the railroad tracks was rapidly filling up and speculated: "there are many attractive home sites in the hills north of the railway. . . perhaps newcomers from New Haven, Middletown, and points further off will prefer the hills to the beaches." Newcomers did, and therein lay the promise and the future of Madison. The people came and the town grew. And it will continue to grow, for at this writing over 1,500 building lots remain.

Would Talcott Bradley, who sold the first shoreline lot to Mrs. Dexter, marvel at what our town has become or would he wish Mrs. Dexter had never fallen in love with Madison?

Warner Lord
Madison, Connecticut
May 1998

One

THE NEW CENTURY
BEGINS
1900–1909

In 1900 Madison was a town of 1,600 inhabitants poised on the edge of dramatic change. The year-round population was stable, having increased by only one hundred since 1830. Residents were mainly farmers and owners of small businesses.

The annual budget for 1900-1901 was $25,310.83, supported by an $11 million tax rate on a grand list of $1,042,749. There were 321 school children attending district schools and Hand Academy. No automobiles disturbed horses and oxen on the town's roadways. Electricity and indoor plumbing were uncommon.

The town was a quiet, quaint, quintessential New England village, but a village destined for enormous and often tumultuous change.

Grace Miner Lippincott, pictured here with her son, Whitney, and her husband, Levi, was a Madison native and renowned poet. She and her family represent the solid New England stock that was the essence of Madison in 1900.

Typical of Madison's citizens at the beginning of the century was S. Arthur Scranton, entrepreneur, builder, and dealer in ice, coal, and groceries. He also served as first selectman at an annual salary of $150.

J. Myron Hull, Madison native, was among those far-sighted individuals who saw potential in developing waterfront land as a summer colony. He and citizens like him were men of vision, with the business sense to determine the direction Madison would take in the coming years.

In 1900 the steeple of the First Congregational Church was completely reconstructed.

These women in front of Memorial Hall are greeting visitors to the 1903 Madison Fair. Fairs had been held annually on the Green for many years—a practice that would continue throughout the century.

Horace Hunter, photographer, undertaker, and furniture salesman, recorded the history of Madison during the first three decades of the century. Many of the photographs in this book are his.

At the turn of the century, Madison was a rural agricultural community. Its life was firmly rooted in the 19th century. These young farmers weighing a load of hay on the scale in front of Peoples Store personify the Madison the summer visitor loved. The church in the background is now the Cafe Lafayette.

Peoples Store was demolished in 1946 to make way for a new brick building. It stood opposite the present firehouse on the south side of the Boston Post Road. It was moved from its original location on the site of Memorial Hall around 1895.

This handsome summer cottage on Island Avenue was built in 1897 for George Augustus Wilcox and family. His daughter, Constance Wilcox Pignatelli, and later his granddaughter, Maria Elena Pignatelli, lived here. The house was sold in 1997. It was among the most elaborate summer cottages to be built and was unique in its design.

Seasonal residents came to populate the newly constructed cottages and enjoy the sun, sand, and solitude. During the years 1900-1909, nine subdivision plans were filed in the town clerk's office. These cottages just east of East Wharf were built to be sold or rented, and soon the seasonal residents began to outnumber permanent residents.

To the north, life went on without the building activity associated with the burgeoning summer colony along the shore. On Summer Hill Road, a farmer and his oxen posed for Horace Hunter in front of the Jonathan Bishop house.

Rockland, the northern-most settled area in town, retained its charm and independence. Home to Stevenses, Oslanders, Blatchleys, and others, it was a farming community. To the left is the Rockland District School, later replaced by a new building that stands today on a knoll on the southwest corner of Route 79 and County Road.

Madison was divided into 13 school districts, each of which supported a one-room school. The Neck District School at the junction of the Post Road and Neck Road was typical. Each served its neighborhood and was supported by the families whose children attended. The schoolhouse survives today as the Schoolhouse Deli.

The Green provided a central location for a wide variety of activities, as it does today. Preserved forever as open space by the founding fathers, it has served as pasture, mosquito-breeding ground, and roadway for north-bound farmers. Its present boundaries and contours were established by 1900. The large trees pictured here were destroyed in the 1938 hurricane.

The Madison Beach Hotel at West Wharf, a former boarding house for shipyard workers, was converted to a hotel for summer visitors. It was advertised as: ". . . a hotel primarily designed for cultured people who desire superior accommodations—and no summer hotel in Connecticut has a more representative clientele."

Madison's intellectual life in 1900 is evidenced by the newly constructed E.C. Scranton Memorial Library, shown here at the dedication celebration on July 2, 1900. It was a gift to the town by Mary Eliza Scranton in memory of her father, Erastus Clark Scranton.

Hand Academy, donated to the town by native son Daniel Hand in 1884, provided deserving young people with an education beyond the eight grades of the district schools. It stood on the present site of Academy Elementary School at the corner of School and Academy Streets.

In 1905 the Boston Post Road was a wide dirt roadway shaded by over-hanging trees. There were no utility poles, no noxious fumes from automobiles, and no street lights. Small stores provided the necessities of life for residents and summer visitors.

On July 4, 1907, a fire, started by a firecracker landing in a wooden rain gutter, destroyed the home of Frank Dunlap and family. The house, located on the south side of Main Street near the site of the present New Haven Savings Bank, was a total loss. The fire led to the founding of Madison Hose Company Number One.

Tuxis Island lies just off the shore at Middle Beach. Legend says this rocky isle is the legacy of strolling giants. It endures as Madison endures. It has seen many changes and will see more. Now home to nesting birds and teenagers in rowboats, it once served as a YMCA camp complete with the house and tents shown in this photograph.

Meigs Tower in the Hammonassett District was a magnet for the Sunday tourist. Modeled on the Mouse Tower on the Rhine River, it was built as a summer home by John Meigs, owner of a clothing store in New Haven. Located on the north side of Cottage Road, no trace of the tower remains today.

At Duck Hole on the Hammonassett River, where River Road crosses into Clinton, stood two mills, a gristmill on the left and a sawmill on the right. These silent relics of the past served as reminders that Madison had a long and productive past. Later the site of a state fish hatchery, nothing remains but a breached dam.

In 1907 the Shoreline Electric Railway Company announced its intention to construct a portion of their trolley line through Madison. As the decade closed, work had begun and tracks were laid through Madison. Apparently a problem developed at Dudley's Crossing in the Hammonassett District as shown in this photograph.

Among the first residents of Madison to take advantage of the new-fangled automobile was Hart Scranton who purchased a 1908 Sears Motor Wagon. Mr. Scranton was Madison's rural mail carrier.

Fishing was still important in Madison, both commercially and for pleasure. These satisfied fishermen are pictured in 1907 with their day's catch of blackfish.

Connecting the Boston Post Road with the shore, Island Avenue represented all that Madison offered the summer resident—quaintness, charm, and tranquillity. This narrow tree-lined lane would grow with the town. In the distance is the familiar chapel, currently home to Madison Youth Services, built in 1884 by the First Congregational Church as a meeting hall.

Two

INFINITE CHARM
1910–1919

By 1915, Madison was a town looking toward a future very different from its past. Summer residents had discovered the town's charm and appeal. The stage was set for the future and Madison's virtues were being extolled to potential visitors and residents throughout the region.

During this decade, the Shore Line Electric Railway and electricity came on the scene, and a World War would take Madison's young men from home.

Edward F. Meyers, a seasonal resident who had an opportunity to experience Madison year-round, wrote a glowing testimonial to "picturesque Old Madison" in the August 19, 1915, issue of the Shore Line Times. Quotes from Mr. Meyer's article have been used in many of the photograph captions in this chapter.

"Its shores are a series of beautiful coves, here and there a grouping of rocks give variety to the picture. Hidden rocks and treacherous shoals are not to be found so that there are the finest and safest of all beaches on the entire shore." It's just right for a pleasant afternoon of boating off Middle Beach near Tuxis Island.

"About a half a mile to the north (of the beach) the Main thoroughfare of the town, Boston Street, is reached and just back of it . . . the hill country is reached. . . woods and hills with here and there lakes and streams of peculiar beauty." Pictured here is the dam at Ninevah Falls on the Hammonassett River in North Madison.

". . . along and near the shore front are modest cottages, some few quite pretentious, all the outgrowth of the charm of its environment without having been fostered by all too prevalent effort of professional 'land boomers' or 'town boosters.' " The scene is Webster Point Road.

"At present there are. . . three or four hundred of the domiciles which together with the two successful hotels of many year's reputation, attract. . . 5,000 people." Pictured is the Hammonassett House hotel which stood immediately west of the mouth of Fence Creek on the location of the present 275 Middle Beach Road.

"A fine Country Club on Middle Beach with its excellent tennis courts and golf links, furnishes amusement for those whose activities are not satisfied with a life on the sand or in the water."

"Its beautiful village Green over which the First Congregational Church stands like a sentinel on guard while the stately elms in quadruple rows with arching branches over the wide, well-kept streets form a picture of infinite charm."

From where "Wall Street intersects Boston Street. . . is to be seen the Post Office while at a convenient point. . . stands a handsome rough stone drinking trough surmounted by an electric light."

"The social life is one of gracious fellowship and is constantly promoted not only by the church, but by concerts, private theatrical lectures, athletic games, etc." Here the Red Cross and a group of soldiers have gathered at 586 Boston Post Road for a ceremony.

"These factors have produced a quiet attractive, livable town, and just such a spot as those in the whirl of a strenuous city life are picturing in their minds. . ." Pictured here is the Boston Post Road in East River near the Guilford town line. The view is west from the Railroad underpass.

"Hand School. . . is an attractive edifice and is largely at the disposal of the community for entertainments,. . . etc. A very neat and artistic little Probate Court House is located next to Memorial Hall and completes the 'group' of public buildings." Note the horse and buggy and the cow grazing on the right.

Even as Mr. Meyers described his idyllic town, changes were evident that would slowly and inexorably bring a transformation to the town. On the beach at Waterbury Avenue, Jack Tweed, summer resident and pilot, created a great stir as he landed his "Headless Biplane" in Long Island Sound in 1913. Hardly dreamed of were the radical changes in transportation to come.

Tuxis Pond lay serenely in the center of town. Tuxis Brook ran from the pond to Long Island Sound and was crossed by means of a simple wooden bridge—the original Tuxis Walkway.

Although the Civil War had been over for nearly 50 years, a small contingent of Civil War veterans still lived in Madison. They posed for a group photograph outside the Congregational church chapel on July 4, 1913.

As the summer colony grew, and more and more cottages were constructed, it became necessary to build new roads. Among them was Seaview Avenue pictured here.

District schools such as the Union District School, which stood where I-95 passes under Horsepond Road, still served the educational needs of the town although increasing population would see them fall into disuse at the beginning of the next decade.

MADISON HONOR ROLL

CHARLES TURANDT
PAUL PAVELKA
CHARLES MINER
J. DOUGLAS DOWD
FRANK LEWANDOWSKI
R. ELLSWORTH BASSETT
HAROLD F. DOWD
IRA S. WATSON
GEORGE DOWD
HERBERT S. WHEDON
LEON WELD
RUDOLPH WILLARD
JOHN H. TWEED
WILLIAM A. FLYNN
LOUIS DOLPH
J. LEROY McCANN
ADELBERT G. BARGDER
GUELOPE RUSSO
BYRON BARGDER
CLAUDIUS PARDEE
STEPHEN F. ZIMMERMAN
RICHARD L. MALO
MARVIN H. GRISWOLD
JOHN F. HEPBURN
FRANK TURANDT
W. JORALEMON WILCOX

FRANK G. KOENIG
CLAUDE H. McALLISTER
WILLIAM MENZEL
CHARLES W. DUDLEY
HERMAN A. DEBENTHAL
HERMAN SCHUMACHER
WILLIAM NELSON
E. LELAND HILL
CHARLES H. HILL
HERBET R. MOODY
ANDREA CASBLE
JOHN GOHLOFF
MILTON E. BURKE
STANLEY W. GRISWOLD
CLARENCE H. BRADLEY
WILLIAM KULVER
SALVATORE BECCIO
ANTONIO DEGRUTO
WILLIAM H. TELFORD
JAY F. CLARK
EDWARD OBERLANDER
IRVING M. BONOFF
LOUIS GLEICHMAN
ALBERT W. ODALL
EARLE W. STONE

ANTHONY R. TSCHOFEN
IRWIN A. RAWSON
GIOVANNI MASICHI
JOHN R. CHITTENDEN
GORDON T. DUNLAP
F. HARRISON DOWD
EARLE G. CALHOUN
THEODORE BACHELER
GRAHAM O. WELLMAN

The town erected a memorial to those residents who had served in World War I. The names on this memorial were later inscribed on marble tablets that are placed in the entryway of Memorial Hall.

During this decade, many of Madison's young men served in the armed forces, including Herman Derenthal who survived the conflict, returned to Madison, and became actively involved in the growth of the community.

The "Madison Army" assembled on the steps of the First Congregational Church in 1918 after a drill session on the Green.

As the decade ended, the town road crew posed for their portrait in front of the First Congregational Church. The horse would soon give way to the automobile and the way of life these men knew would begin to change. Pictured from left to right are the following: James Pickett, Arthur Bartlett, Darwell Conklin (driving), and Harry Parmelee.

In 1915 the Young Men's Club of Madison, several of whom are pictured here in their basketball uniforms, published a booklet entitled *Madison Illustrated* in which they proclaimed the charms of Madison. They wrote that "Madison cannot help but grow steadily in prosperity and become an ideal place to live."

Several serious trolley accidents increased public concern for the safety of this new form of mass transit. By the middle of the next decade, the Shore Line Electric Railway would fall into bankruptcy and disappear from the scene.

In 1919 Madison Hose Company Number One purchased its first mechanized fire apparatus. This Model T Ford fire truck cost approximately $3,100. It was later associated with the only line-of-duty death in department history when a fireman laying hose across the railroad tracks was struck by a train.

Three

SIGNIFICANT CHANGES
1920–1929

The period between 1920 and 1929 was marked by significant changes resulting from the increased development in town. Thirty-seven subdivision maps had been filed in the years between 1887 and 1929. Madison was growing economically, in population, and in complexity. Schools were becoming crowded, new roads were being built, new services demanded, the grand list was growing, and the annual budget expanding.

The 1920s were a decade of growth and change. The past was giving way to the future. Important issues relative to beaches and schools confronted the town. Increasing automobile traffic brought demands for traffic control.

The trolley disappeared and Hammonassett State Park became a major attraction. And as Madison celebrated its 100th anniversary as a town apart from Guilford, a great Depression settled on the country.

At the end of the last decade, the district schools were either over-crowded or had fallen into disuse. All district schools, with the exception of the Rockland School, were closed and a new school was constructed. The new school, named Hand Consolidated School, opened on March 27, 1922, with a single room for each grade K-12.

In 1923 the old Rockland School was demolished and this building erected in its place. Eventually it too was closed and all pupils attended the Hand Consolidated School. The building exists today as a home.

The Woods District School was located at the junction of Green Hill Road and Horsepond Road on the Woods District Green. It is pictured here in 1921, the last year of its operation.

Madison's first school bus was purchased to transport children to the new consolidated school. One long-time resident recalled that often, it was necessary for pupils to get out of the bus in muddy or slippery weather to help push it up a hill!

Hammonassett State Park opened in July 1921, creating Connecticut's largest state park. Its setting was Madison's fine mile-long stretch of sandy beach.

The park featured day-use facilities for bathing and picnicking, and long- and short-term camping facilities. As the park prospered, a new commercial district grew up nearby along Route One. Tourist courts and commercial establishments proliferated, catering to the needs of tourists and park visitors.

In 1921, the building on the right, Madison's second movie theater, was constructed for Charles Bonoff. In addition to a theater, it contained two stores, and served as a basketball court until a sloping floor was added. The theater was unique on the shoreline as one the few remaining early movie theaters until its closing in April 1998.

In 1921 the Visiting Nurse Association of Madison was established to provide health care for the schools. The town voted to support the organization with a grant of $1,000. Miss Evelyn Law was hired as school nurse. The photograph shows her with a group of students practicing first aid in the health office, which was located atop Hand Consolidated School.

In 1922 the Methodist church was sold to Mr. and Mrs. Carrington to be converted to an inn. Built by Congregationalists who left the First Congregational Church in a dispute over the location of a proposed new church, it was sold to the Methodist Society in 1839. The Methodist congregation dwindled to the point where maintaining a building was not possible.

In a barn behind her house on the Boston Post Road, Constance Wilcox Pignatelli produced plays. These were an outgrowth of plays she produced in her garden in earlier years. The plays were well received in the area and represented the beginning of the summer theater movement in the United States. The Playbarn evolved into the Jitney Players, a touring company which traveled extensively.

The Jitney Players were formed in 1923 by Bushnell Cheney and his wife, Alice Keating Cheney. In "Jezebel," the Jitney Player's combination truck and collapsible stage, the players traveled from Canada to Mexico presenting summer theater productions. Among the Jitney Players were many well-known actors, including Monty Woolly, Ethel Barrymore, and Hume Cronin.

The trolley still ran regularly through Madison but its days were numbered. This photograph shows trolley cars passing each other in Madison center. The Methodist church is shown in the background. By the end of the decade, the Shore Line Electric Railway was bankrupt and only the tracks remained.

In 1926, Madison celebrated its centennial with a gala parade complete with marching bands and floats of every description. The parade is shown here passing the intersection of Wall Street and the Boston Post Road.

In 1923, after the completion of Hand Consolidated School, Lee Academy was moved to its present location to provide more playground space for Hand pupils. Originally constructed as a private school on the southeast corner of Neck Road and the Boston Post Road, Lee Academy has been moved four times.

During this decade, eight new roads, including Grove Avenue, were accepted as town roads. During the same period, 11 roads which had fallen into disuse in the northern part of town were abandoned.

Automobile traffic had increased to the extent that parking regulations were established for the business district between Wall Street and Tuxis Brook. Parking in summer was limited to 45 minutes. Vernon Willard was appointed special constable and traffic officer in 1923. By 1927, parking regulations were amended to prohibit driving on the sidewalk except to make deliveries.

In 1920, the Madison Historical Society purchased the Allis-Bushnell house at 853 Boston Post Road. The Society had been founded three years earlier in 1917. The photograph is dated 1924.

In 1927 Howard Kelsey was elected first selectman. He served until his death in 1952 when he was succeeded by Gordon Peery.

During this decade, summer cottages like these at Circle Beach were constructed in increasing numbers. The first steps to control the phenomenon came in 1925 when the town established the office of building inspector. In 1927 the first building ordinances were enacted.

On the crest of High Hill in North Madison stands a reproduction French farmhouse. It was built in 1929 for Russell C. Northam, a broker from Hartford, as a country estate. Known locally as the "Silly Putty House" in honor of a later resident, it is now part of the Legend Hill Condominiums.

In 1897 George C. Field arrived in Madison and began working as a carpenter and undertaker. By 1928 the Field Company was a respected and prosperous construction company located on Wall Street. This photograph, dated 1928, shows the familiar Field Company building on Wall Street.

The Field Company built many of the residential and commercial buildings in Madison, including the Hull Building on Wall Street. Pictured here in August 1928 are J. Myron Hull, William Seward Hull, and Leland Hull in front of their newly completed building.

Four

CALM BEFORE THE STORM
1930–1939

"Beautiful Shore Line Town Slowly Succumbing to Devastating Modernism Lives Happily in Recollections of Days When Life Was Not Simply Dollar Chase"

Thus began an article in the Sunday, July 8, 1934, issue of the *New Haven Register*. The story contrasted Madison in the 1860s as described by Jane Bushnell Shepherd in her book *Going to Madison in the Sixties*, with Madison in 1934, the sophisticated Madison which had become "the discovery of the decade, among the leisurely wealthy."

The Boston Post Road was described as a "pulsing artery of traffic (that) beats through the town. One after another, the Boston bound cars streak past under... interlocking elms."

Of the fine old homes on Boston Street the reporter wrote: "lovely old houses on the street preserve a pathetic dignity, even though they have been turned into inns, and yarn shops, and beauty shops."

In 1932 the Boston Post Road was the major highway connecting New York and Boston. It was described by the *New Haven Register* as a "dangerous knife" cutting through the heart of Madison. Commercial traffic, tourist traffic, and local traffic combined to create serious problems. Note the police officer patrolling the business district on his motorcycle.

At East Wharf the last of the fish houses recalled the halcyon days of fishing and shipping. East Wharf had become a ruin of dark rocks, crumbling into the sea: "To see it at all you (had) to ask permission of one of the beautiful white cottages. . . for the houses of the Summer People stand shoulder to shoulder."

The tourist vied with the property-owning summer resident for Madison's charms. Townspeople converted chicken coops into tourist accommodations. Uncle Dud's Cabins, Dowd's Modern Cabins, the Wayside Cabins on Route One, and Applehurst Cabins on Neck Road promised two weeks of sun, sand, and solitude.

In 1933 the simple wooden bridge that had spanned the Hammonassett River at Ninevah Falls in North Madison was replaced by a modern concrete structure. Route 80 now crosses into Killingworth at this point.

In 1933, S. Archie Holdridge, Vocational Agriculture teacher in the Guilford and Madison public schools, formed the Guilford-Madison Chapter of the Future Farmers of America. The charter members had their picture taken on the front steps of Hand Consolidated School. Mr. Holdridge is in the second row center. In 1937 the group would hold their first annual Future Farmers Fair.

Each summer Hammonassett State Park was filled to overflowing with campers and sunbathers who came from the steaming cities to feast on fried clams, clam chowder, and hot dogs.

The country club on Middle Beach Road filled the days of the summer resident with tennis, golf, and an endless round of parties. Life was good beside the sea in Madison, Connecticut. The country club building, located just west of number 78 Middle Beach Road, was destroyed in the 1938 hurricane.

In 1937, plans were made to build a new post office on the corner of Wall Street, directly opposite the old one situated in the Monroe Building on the south side of Main Street. The Wilcox house which stood on the site of the proposed post office was moved up Wall Street to number 11.

The new post office was completed in 1938. One of its notable features was a WPA mural in the lobby portraying the harvesting of seaweed for use as fertilizer. As this book is being written, the postal service is considering plans for a new building.

As summer cottages, like these on Neck Road, filled the shore lands, property owners became increasingly concerned that if growth was not controlled, the town would quickly be overbuilt. In 1931 the first zoning regulations were proposed. From that date on, Madison exercised careful control of residential and commercial building.

The heart and soul of Madison was still its citizens. Among them was Walter Polson, affectionately known as "Pop" Polson. He is on the right in the last row with the 1930 baseball team. The picture was taken on the front steps of Hand Consolidated School.

This photograph of the Stevens Inn on Main Street captures the essence of Madison in 1938: quaint, charming, quintessential New England. Madison's future as a resort town was well established. Zoning ordinances assured control over future development, and the town's attractiveness would insure continued growth. The residents worked to protect the town's character from the pressures of change.

In 1931, the balcony was removed from Memorial Hall. In 1935, the town voted not to spend $2,500 for a heating system. In 1938, $18,000 was appropriated to remodel Memorial Hall for use as town offices, and in 1939, the town clerk's office and probate records were moved into the newly renovated building. They would remain until the completion of the Town Campus in 1995.

This photograph shows the hanger at Griswold's Airport on Airline Road (later called New Road). The airplane is a Bird biplane belonging to Jack Carrington. The airport, located where I-95 passes under New Road, began operation in the late 1920s and moved to its present location on Boston Post Road in 1931. In 1998, the airport was sold for commercial development.

As the summer of 1938 blended into autumn, heavy rains soaked Madison leaving large puddles on the Green. This view is looking south toward the Jonathan S. Wilcox house on the Boston Post Road.

On September 27, 1938, a devastating hurricane tore through Madison. Over half the magnificent spruce trees on the Green were destroyed. Helen Marsh wrote in her diary that: "Madison would never be the same again."

Elizabeth Wright's restaurant, Wagon Wheels, in the Hammonassett District was severely damaged by the storm. It was repaired and reopened soon after.

The Boston Post Road east of Wall Street and the library was impassable. Once-stately elm trees were scattered like giant jackstraws.

At the height of the storm, an enormous tidal wave struck. The Madison Golf Course was littered with debris left by the receding water.

More than one shorefront cottage was reduced to a splintered ruin by the force of the tidal wave. Cottages were knocked from their foundations and in some cases washed far from their original sites. Some houses were totally destroyed while neighboring houses received only minor damage.

Clean-up began immediately as ruined buildings were dismantled and replaced. This scene on Middle Beach clearly shows the devastation created along the shore.

The 1930s ended quietly. The hurricane was a distant memory. Hand Consolidated School had been enlarged by the addition of classrooms and a gymnasium,where the 1939 football team had its picture taken.

Five

THE QUIET YEARS
1940–1949

The decade of the 1940s was a time of relative quiet after the activity of the 1930s. WW II took Madison's young people away from home. The town continued its growth but at a slower pace. Route One still functioned as the major traffic artery, but there were rumors that it would be relocated to the north away from the business district.

By the end of the decade, the school population had risen to 588, the highest in the history of the town.

Howard Kelsey began his seventh term as first selectman in 1941. The town purchased its first voting machines in 1948, retiring the ballot box forever. As the decade closed, the town created a building committee to plan a school to house all the elementary students of the town. For the first time in its history, the town would purchase land and build a school.

In 1940, the world was on the brink of a second world war, and many in the Hand High graduating class of 1940 would serve in the Armed Forces. Madison had 2,200 residents as the decade began, and there would be three thousand at its end. Agriculture was still important although development was beginning to spread north of the railroad tracks.

In 1948 Clinton Theis filed a subdivision plan for Hamilton Drive in the East Wharf area. The homes, comparable to the one pictured here, were to be year-round rather than seasonal. The era of residential development had begun, and would spread northward as the century progressed.

Madison's business district still retained its small-town character. As a result of the first zoning regulations in 1932, commercial development was confined to the central business district, and the eastern and western extremes of the Boston Post Road.

As the 1940s drew to a close, Michael Doerrer, a German immigrant, gathered with his wife, Amelia, daughter Elizabeth, and grandson Stephen, for a family portrait. The Doerrers were representative of the German families that settled in Madison early in the century. Their family farm on Duck Hole Road was later abandoned to make way for the Connecticut Turnpike.

In 1942, Jay Clark, town engineer and surveyor, photographed commercial establishments along the Boston Post Road from the Guilford Line to the Clinton Line. Cutler's restaurant located on the bank of the East River was typical of the small businesses found along the Post Road.

Hilda's Diner, located where the Cumberland Farms store now stands, catered to the large volume of truck and tourist traffic on Route One. Operated in the 1940s by Hilda Wagner, it was a local landmark. In 1949, it was moved to Durham and then to New York State.

At the eastern edge of town near the Clinton town line, the Hammonassett commercial district continued to develop. Gas stations, restaurants, and tourist courts flourished. The Deluxe Cabins were demolished to make way for the present Mobil station.

In the 1940s, there were 26 gas stations and garages in Madison and North Madison. The Madison Garage, located on the site of the present New Haven Savings Bank and Courtyard, had opened in 1909. It survived until the 1960s when the business moved to Guilford and the building was demolished.

This photograph shows the First Congregational Church, the Webb House (later demolished to make way for the Congregational church house), and a tennis court on the site of the present Academy Elementary School playground. Recreation programs for Madison residents were first funded in 1945 when the town voted to appropriate $680 to provide recreation for boys and girls.

Among Madison's young men to answer their country's call during WW II was Peter Casula, later the town's ambulance driver. This photograph is dated January 2, 1943.

Four other young men who served in the Armed Forces during WW II had their picture taken on Main Street. Listed from left to right are as follows: Robert Argyros, Peter Gallagher, John Doerrer, and Louis Argyros.

In 1943 the town voted that $400 be used to erect an honor roll of Madison men and women serving in the Armed Forces. The honor roll was removed in 1947 when the town appropriated money for the American Legion to construct a lounge in their building on Bradley Road to serve as a veteran's memorial.

In 1949, the Madison Grange erected a hall on Bradley Road on land leased from the town. Lumber for construction of the hall was salvaged from Civilian Conservation Corps camp on Copse Road. The CCC buildings were dismantled by members of the Grange and stored in the horse sheds behind Lee Academy until the hall was built.

In the 1940s, the number of pre-school children in Madison was twice the number of residents over the age of 65. Increasing numbers of children created a need for more classroom space. In 1947, a school building committee was established to plan for a new elementary school. This photograph was taken in 1942 at Seaview Avenue Beach.

Pictured is Dr. Robert H. Brown, superintendent of schools, entering the side door of Hand Consolidated School. He was hired as superintendent in 1942 and held the post until his retirement in 1969.

On September 10, 1946, Madison celebrated "Dr. Rindge Day" in honor of Dr. Milo P. Rindge shown above on the steps of the chapel with his daughter, Dr. Mila Rindge. More than one hundred of the seven hundred children delivered during his 40 years of practice in Madison attended the celebration, which included a parade and reception. Dr. Rindge was characterized as a "beloved physician, public-spirited citizen, and Christian gentleman."

The People's Store, which had served Madison since the turn of the century, was demolished in 1946 and replaced by a new brick building. Its passing underscored the fact that Madison has always been an evolving town. Each new decade brought carefully considered change that enhanced the quality of life for residents—permanent and seasonal.

In North Madison, Roland Stevens served the Rockland community with his "Sunrise Fine Food Store." The store still stands beside Route 79 in Rockland reminding us that Rockland is an important part of Madison. Mr. Stevens's recollections, entitled Pot Skimmin's, describe mid-century life in North Madison. The photograph was taken by Jay Clark in 1942.

Each September, S. Archie Holdridge, vocational agriculture teacher at Hand Consolidated School, directed the annual fair of the Guilford-Madison Chapter of the Future Farmers of America. This photograph is dated 1949.

The Future Farmers parade included the local fire departments, bands, the American Legion, police and scout groups, floats, farm equipment, and decorated automobiles. To the left in this 1949 photograph can be seen Hilda's Diner and Molnar's Garage, later to become the home of Madison Hose Company Number One.

The Future Farmer's Fair was held on the grounds of Hand Consolidated School. Exhibits were set up on the school grounds and in the building itself.

Featured at the fair were pulling contests with horses and homemade tractors, agricultural exhibits, and band performances.

Six
A FLURRY OF ACTIVITY
1950–1959

The 1950s were years of frantic growth. Schools were planned and built. The town was suddenly divided by a four-lane highway opening the door to a flood of new residents. A frenzy of construction activity resulted. The pre-eminence of the seasonal visitor over the permanent resident was about to end.

The town began the decade with a population of three thousand, twice that of 1900. The schools were filled to overflowing, and classes spilled over into Lee Academy and the Grange Hall. A new school opened in 1950 only to require an addition two years later. In 1954 the town purchased land for a new high school and another elementary school.

In 1951 there were 629 pupils in the pupils schools. By the decade's end there would be 1,511.

Another war would claim Madison's young men and women, the Exchange Club would be formed, the Planning and Zoning Commission would develop the first comprehensive plan for the town, and toll-dodging trucks would disrupt local traffic and frustrate town officials.

As the decade opened, Peck's Poultry Farm stood on Route 79, just north of the railroad tracks. One of the last vestiges of Madison's agricultural past, its days were numbered. By the decade's end, no trace would be left to mark its existence.

S. Archie Holdridge still taught Vocational Agriculture at Hand Consolidated School. The Future Farmers of America held their annual fair and competed in a variety of activities on the state level. Mr. Holdridge is on the far right in the second row. His son, Dale, is in the middle of the back row. The last Future Farmers Fair was held in 1958.

New Road was a country lane devoid of houses. No hint of the future appears in this photograph. There is not even a glimpse of the upheaval and change that would be produced when New Road was intersected by the new turnpike.

In 1949, the town meeting voted to purchase land on Island Avenue for an elementary school. This photograph, taken on April 16, 1950, shows the first stages of construction. Island Avenue School was dedicated on October 25, 1950. It was the first of five schools the town would build during the next two decades.

The growing population soon created downtown parking problems, so a committee was formed to study the issue. The result was the Charles Woolsey Scranton Memorial Parking Lot. The land was a gift to the town from four local residents. Pictured here is Alice Scranton Milliken cutting the ribbon at the dedication of the parking lot in August 1952.

Gordon Peery, Charles Genesius, Otis Chapman, and Fred Holbrook preside over the opening of the new telephone dialing system. All phone calls were previously handled by operators in the Monroe Building. To familiarize students with the new system, Hand High School offered training in the use of the dial telephone.

In 1957, Main Street was uncrowded and the center esplanade had not been added. The buildings in this picture were later destroyed in a fire. Of the businesses pictured, only Jolly's Drugstore remains.

A new Chevrolet could still be purchased on Main Street but not for long. Town meeting minutes record a flurry of activity as citizens confronted new issues related to increased population and demands for services. The Public Beach Committee, High School Building Committee, and an elected Board of Police Commissioners were created to deal with some of these issues.

In 1956, the State of Connecticut prepared to construct the Connecticut Turnpike. This section of Copse Road would never look the same again. The two houses in the foreground of this photograph taken on March 11, 1956, were moved elsewhere as the Connecticut Turnpike cut a swath through town.

A year later, on May 28, 1957, the section of Copse Road shown in the previous photograph looked like this. The Connecticut Turnpike construction had begun, and Madison would be changed forever.

Madison's native rock was blasted away to make a passage for the thousands who would use the Hammonassett Connector as their gateway to Hammonassett State Park. This view is from the Boston Post Road looking north.

The East River was diverted from its course, and a new channel was dredged near the site of the present-day Beebe Marine seen in the left background of this photograph. To the right is the Fowler Nursing Home, on the Guilford bank of the East River.

Where Peck Farm stood, the concrete ribbon grew, opening Madison to the world. The predominance of the summer colony and the influx of summer residents would give way to a growing year-round population, as families sought Madison's desirable atmosphere. In the right center of this photograph is the bridge over the Hammonasset River at Duck Hole.

The Connecticut Turnpike opened on January 2, 1958. The vacant land seen here near the Mungertown interchange would soon fill with homes. Toll-dodging trucks created traffic

problems and frequently became stuck under the Mungertown railroad underpass. The next decades would bring a building boom as farmlands were opened for development.

Land was purchased for an elementary-high school complex, and construction began on the Copse Road Elementary School, now J. Milton Jeffrey Elementary School, which opened in 1958. The High School Building Committee immediately began to plan for the construction of Daniel Hand High School on the same property.

The 1957 prediction that the hills to the north of the railroad tracks would attract future residents was about to come true. The Hoerndler Farm on Horsepond Road would disappear as developments filled the landscape luring seekers of solitude and country charm. Madison had not lost her appeal, and she was now open to the world.

This newly constructed three-bedroom ranch house on Green Hill Road sold for $14,800 in April 1959. It was advertised as close to the thruway with construction by a reputable builder. Excellent financing was available.

In 1952, Mr. Johnson took a picture of his fifth grade class at Hand Consolidated School. By 1956, enrollment had increased by 40% more than the enrollment in 1946. Mr. Johnson's students found themselves among the last to graduate from Hand Consolidated School. In 1961, the new Daniel Hand High School was dedicated.

As construction of the Connecticut Turnpike began in 1956, the New Haven Water Company was completing a tunnel to carry water from Lake Hammonassett Reservoir, located north of Route 80 in North Madison, to Lake Gaillard in North Branford. A new dam was constructed obliterating forever the stone dam at Ninevah Falls.

Despite the pressures on the town, the elusive charm that endeared Madison to her residents remained. There was a quaintness in her old homes, shaded streets, and sandy beaches. She was still a town of wooded landscapes and solid Yankee character.

Seven

GROWING PAINS
1960–1969

In January 1960, the Connecticut Turnpike was two years old. Toll revenues were $13,101,265 for the year. The population of Madison grew from 3,078 in 1950 to 4,567 in 1960—a 48% increase. By 1970, the population would double to 9,768. During the same period, turnpike toll revenues would double as well.

At the beginning of the decade there were 1,080 pupils in the public schools; in 1964 there were 1,573 and by 1969, there were 2,781 students.

Before the decade was over the voters of the town would accept 64 new roads. The growth was fueled by the Connecticut Turnpike which offered easy access to Madison's charms.

Slowly the number of permanent residents surpassed the number of seasonal residents. Madison moved beyond its role as a summer resort. In 1957 the *Shore Line Times* speculated—"Perhaps newcomers from New Haven, Middletown, and points further off will prefer the hills to the beaches." They did and therein lay the future of Madison. Summer Hill Road, Opening Hill Road, Horsepond, Route 79, and Route 80 became the thoroughfares leading to the new residential developments.

In 1960 a town meeting voted 430-215 to purchase the Surf Club property for $250,000, thus adding a substantial building and several hundred feet of public beach to the town's desirable assets.

Early in the decade, Gordon Peery, first selectman, Jay Clark, and Eugene Keyarts joined Winfred Chittenden and Edwin Bartlett of Guilford to perambulate the boundaries of Madison for the last time. A tradition since Madison's incorporation in 1826, the selectman regularly walked the boundaries of the town insuring that the stone boundary markers were all intact and in good repair.

An Exciting New Design
The Contemporary Raised Ranch
Riverside Terrace
In Madison

Featuring 3 spacious bedrooms, 2½ baths, living room, dining room, two fireplaces. Two-car garage, finished recreation room, laundry room. Sliding glass door to a cantilevered sun deck. Double windows and screens. General Electric P7 self-cleaning range, dishwasher and disposal.

All On A Beautiful Acre For Only **$26,400**

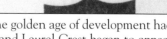

In 1961, 13 new roads were accepted by the town meeting. The golden age of development had begun. Names such as Riversedge Farms, Beechwoods Drive, and Laurel Crest began to appear on the town map. The new developments offered easy access to the Turnpike, running brooks, colonial stone walls, and large acre lots—all the elements of life in the country.

In 1962, Main Street was still much as it had been. Stores were small and met most needs of the populace. There was no center esplanade. A hint of small-town character remained.

The house belonging to Mrs. Thomas Jolly, that stood on the northeast corner of the intersection of the Boston Post Road and Route 79, was taken down in 1962 to make way for a First National Grocery Store. CVS Pharmacy now occupies this site.

The Madison Garage was demolished to make way for the Madison Mall in 1968. Established in 1909, the garage had been a landmark for nearly 60 years.

From the ruins of the Madison Garage, grew the next generation of Madison businesses. The showroom for the latest model Chevrolet was replaced by a bank, specialty stores, and a courtyard with benches and trees.

In 1960 the last senior class graduated from Hand Consolidated School. The school was replaced by a new high school named Daniel Hand High School. The old building became the Madison Junior High School housing grades 6-8, and later the Academy Elementary School.

Construction began on the new high school in 1959, and by August 1960 the building was nearing completion.

In 1963, land was purchased in North Madison for school construction, and in 1965, work began on the High Hill Elementary School, now known as Ryerson School. The building was completed in 1965.

Planning for a new middle school began in 1968 and construction of the Robert H. Brown Middle School began in 1969. Building committee members, town officials, and Dr. Robert Brown (fourth from the left) are shown at the groundbreaking ceremony.

As the central business district evolved and the school system grew, the town was struggling with other matters. The purchase of the Surf Club property in 1960 was followed by the purchase of the 45-acre Garvan property for $500,000 in 1966. The Garvan section, shown in the background of this view, included a large house and barn.

Less romantic town business included the purchase of property for a new waste disposal site on Ridge Road adjacent to the old town dump. The photograph shows first selectman Robert Adams (pointing), town officials, and John B. Janssen (center back) discussing the purchase of land owned by Mr. Janssen.

First Selectman Robert Adams commissioned a town seal to be designed by Robert Terrill. The seal depicted early activities of the town, including shipbuilding, fishing, and farming.

Following several years of legal wrangling, the town determined that the Green belonged to the Congregational church and was therefore tax-exempt.

The Webb house which stood beside the First Congregational Church was demolished in 1961 and a new building was constructed to meet the space needs of the church. Here Rev. Franklin Bower (left), Associate Pastor Charles Gelbach, and Herbert Clark of the George C. Field Company officiate at the laying of the corner stone of the new building.

In 1968, the Lutheran Church of Madison launched an expansion program. The church had been built in 1955 with 60 confirmed members. Increasing membership made expansion of the building necessary.

The building boom continued. In 1968 this newly constructed nine-room house on a half-acre lot was listed at $42,500. Taxes were estimated to be $500. The house featured electric heat, two-car attached garage, paved driveway, and seeded lawn.

In 1969, Dr. Robert H. Brown retired after 27 years as superintendent of schools.

Constance Wilcox Pignatelli, Grace Miner Lippincott, Nellie Scranton, Mary Scranton Evarts, and Marion Wellman, charter members of the Madison Historical Society, celebrated the Society's 50th anniversary in 1967.

By decade's end, the central business district had changed radically. There were two major supermarkets—A & P and First National Stores. A service station stood where Hilda's Diner had once offered breakfast to hungry truckers. A new bank, Union Trust, stood on the corner of Meigs Avenue and Boston Post Road, and the library had completed its first addition.

Eight

New Challenges
1970–1979

Turnpike-generated growth continued to cause controversy, as town services were expanded rapidly in the 70s. Students and senior citizens, zoning and land preservation, a new police station, and the Garvan property addition to the Surf Club, were all new concerns.

In contrast, the Bicentennial celebration renewed interest in the town's heritage. By the end of the decade, a second voting district was established to accommodate the residents of North Madison. The "Pines"—the small triangle of land where Horsepond Road meets Route 79 and beachgoers were wont to stop for a shady lunch—no longer defined the village limits. Picnic tables and cooking grates disappeared as Oakwood, Princess Pines, and Mendingwall joined the town.

Members of the Garden Club of Madison volunteer their time and talent year-round to create an attractive town. In summer, barrels of flowers line the Main Street median, one of the group's early projects. In winter, evergreens and red bows will appear in their place. Throughout Madison, similar small pockets of landscaping are part of the Club's Civic Beautification Program.

One of several active service clubs that benefit the town, the Exchange Club supports many projects for the youth of Madison. The annual Easter Egg Hunt is one of the most exciting for both participants and their parents cheering from the sidelines.

The Hammonassett School was established by local backers as a private secondary day school. Its liberal arts/college preparatory curriculum reflected the contemporary trend toward open classes and ungraded evaluation. The gymnasium, shown here under construction, was one of three buildings nestled in the low hills off the Hammonassett Connector. When the school closed, the campus became the town government center.

The new middle school which opened in February 1971 was named in honor of Dr. Robert H. Brown, who had retired after 27 years. The middle school band and town dignitaries listen to Dr. Brown speaking at the dedication ceremony in front of the school. The former middle school became Academy Elementary School. That year, 3,049 students attended town schools.

Built early in this century, the North Madison Schoolhouse, located just south of the Route 80 circle, served the surrounding area until the schools were consolidated. The school building was then remodeled to serve as a firehouse. In the 1970s, it was torn down to make room for a new, larger North Madison firehouse.

Baseball and football both benefited when Harold Strong, on the left throwing out a ball, donated money to construct Strong Field at the Surf Club. The field provided a much-needed home for the Hand High football team. The addition of powerful lights made it possible for Friday night football games to become a favorite town sporting event.

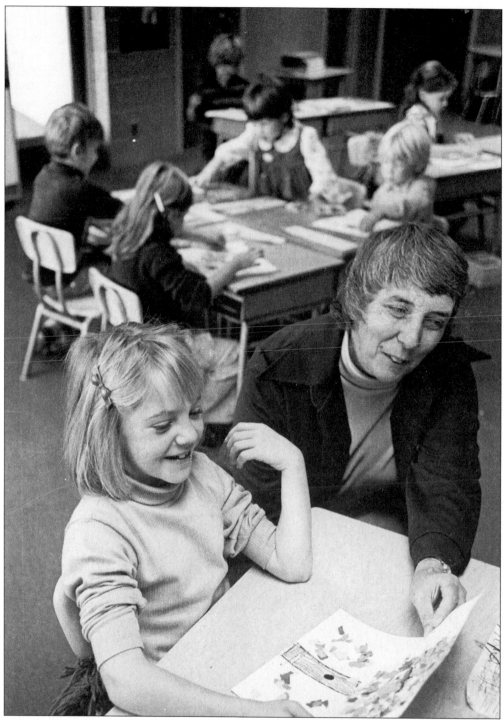

Kathleen Ryerson, principal of the High Hill School in North Madison, was a dedicated educator who maintained a close rapport with her students. Here she admires a student's work. High Hill was later renamed in her honor. Mrs. Ryerson also wrote a history of Madison for elementary students entitled *A Brief History of Madison*.

A pilot-in-training inspects his plane before taxiing down the runway at Griswold Airport. The 70s saw the peak of air traffic in Madison, when private planes rented tie-downs by the day or month, and the Beach and Recreation Department offered flying lessons.

After working 18 months to write regulations meeting both local needs and State Commission requirements, the charter Inland Wetlands Commission is sworn in by First Selectwoman Vera Dallas (left) in 1974. Like all town commissions, Inland Wetlands members donate their time and expertise. They also are expected to take courses in the commission's areas of concern.

The Madison Red Cross and the town used the First Congregational Church house as a shelter during emergencies. Here, residents leave the shelter safe and dry after a hurricane swept through town.

Policing a growing population with its attendant traffic and other "urban" problems had long since exceeded the capabilities of two part-time constables on bicycles. By 1974, the town had a full-time police department, but it had outgrown the facilities of the yellow brick, "powder house" building next to Memorial Hall. This new police station was built that year on Old Route 79.

Like other area churches that were becoming cramped, St. Margaret's Roman Catholic Church underwent major expansion and remodeling in 1975. Scaffolding adorns the tower as part of the belfry is removed, a ramp access added, and additional space for the expanding congregation provided.

In 1977, a beloved minister, who had served Madisonians in many quiet ways, retired after 36 years. Following his church farewell, the town held Franklin Bower Day on the Green to show its love and appreciation. Organizations presented awards and gifts, while groups such as the Nautical Wheelers, shown here square dancing, provided entertainment.

First Selectwoman Vera Dallas, in full colonial costume, rides in a horse-drawn carriage down the Boston Post Road as part of the 1976 Bicentennial Parade. Coinciding with its own 150th Anniversary, Madison participated in the celebration with special fervor. Activities included some of ongoing value, such as the architectural survey of historic buildings and the designation of the Green area as a Historic District.

One of the highlights of the bicentennial year was the Spirit of '76, a pageant depicting historic events. Directed by Margaret Jennings, the cast included over two hundred townspeople of all ages and was performed at Daniel Hand High School. Money raised was used to purchase playground equipment for Jeffrey Elementary School and Academy Elementary School.

The historic Madison Beach Hotel, formerly named the Flower Hotel, with its attached Wharf Restaurant, was long the summer home of visitors returning each year, often to the same rooms. The restaurant served mainly the hotel guests.

An early morning fire in 1978 did more than $100,000 worth of damage and destroyed the restaurant. The timely response of Madison's volunteer firemen managed to save the adjacent hotel building. The restaurant was rebuilt and later the hotel was remodeled.

The Holly Park House at the Surf Club was the town's first senior citizen center. Limited to summer use, it provided a place for senior activities, meetings, and the Senior Citizens Club, including the Club "Kitchen Band," a fixture in local parades. In 1985, a hurricane so damaged the building that it was abandoned, and the fire department burned it for fire-fighting practice.

Temple Beth Tikvah was one of a growing number of religious houses in Madison. Richard Ottenheimer, building committee member (on the right), and the construction supervisor are seen in front of the partially completed structure on Durham Road.

Town history would not be complete without acknowledging the numerous craft groups whose talents enrich the community. These members of the First Congregational Women's League create hand-made items year-round. Funds raised at their annual fair benefit many local and international programs. Eliza Sylvada (center), a Madison native, was the first League member to reach her 100th birthday.

Nine

THE BUILDING BOOM
1980–1989

The 1980 census counted 14,000 Madison citizens. There were 3,197 students in the public schools. A residential construction boom produced major growth in the town. Classrooms were added to Jeffrey Elementary School and Daniel Hand High School.

In 1985, Hurricane Gloria brought the town to a temporary standstill while residents coped without running water or electricity—some for several weeks.

The town also acquired a Marine Patrol Boat, a Harbormaster, and its first official Town Historian—Charlotte Evarts.

It is 1981, and the "back" shopping area is surrounded by trees. The Meigswood office complex and a landscaped Scranton Park are yet to be. The former entrance to the Union Trust Bank has not been realigned, and the businesses facing south behind the Post Road are few.

Madison Hardware, that haven for weekend do-it-yourselfers as well as serious builders, "just 88 steps from the post office," offered household gifts along with helpful advice. Originally a boarding house and hotel, it had been a hardware store for most of this century when it closed in 1992.

Another old friend, Camp's Food Market, closed during this decade, to the regret of many. Noted for its excellent meats, it was the last food store in town to offer that genteel and most appreciated service, home grocery delivery.

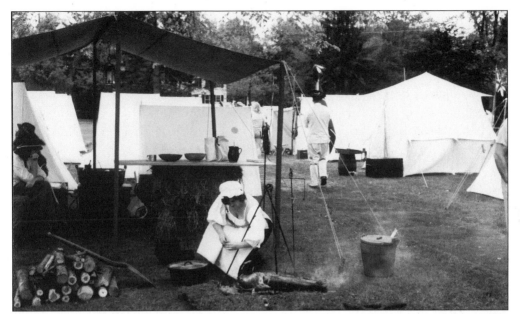

Madison was invaded in 1982 by a troop of "authentic" and knowledgeable Revolutionary War re-enactors and their families. Tents sprang up on the Green and meals were cooked over open fires. In addition to their "living history" roles, they recreated "the Battle for Madison" at Garvan Point. (The colonists won!)

The Deacon John Grave House survived the family whose home it had been since 1685. Recognizing its historic significance, a foundation was formed to preserve and restore the house. Outside scaffolding was a visual indication of the major renovations made to the entire structure. The house is open to the public on a regular basis.

Lenny and Joe's Fish Tale—seasonal, open air, and mainly take-out—flourished with good food and community service. Now open year-round, with indoor seating as well as picnic tables, the restaurant supports community charities by donating selected days' proceeds to a variety of causes.

Nick's Restaurant, touted for its hamburgers, was home to local wags who sat in this front window mentally rearranging the letters on the movie marquee across the street. They would then scale the building and change the words—to the amusement and shock of late night traffic! The building survived the downtown fire in 1985, but Nick's went out of business shortly thereafter.

East Wharf is a reminder of Madison's past as a shipbuilding center. The last shipyard was destroyed by fire at the end of the 19th century, and the wharf was reduced to little more than a pile of rocks by subsequent hurricanes. Rebuilt in the 1980s after Hurricane Gloria, it is now a favorite fishing spot.

A pavilion at East Wharf offers shaded benches overlooking the water and the new walkway out to the rebuilt pier. Night lighting shows off the outlines of the structure designed by Yale architecture students. A new bathhouse and parking area further enhances one of Madison's three town beaches.

Building a major addition on the east side of the E.C. Scranton Memorial Library involved coordinating several floor levels and a major disruption of working space. Librarian Sandy Long negotiates through the construction to keep the library functioning as one of the state's most used public libraries.

Known as the Goddard Project in honor of Richard Goddard, the Scranton Library corner was re-landscaped and paved with decorative bricks. The project highlighted the new library entrance between the old and new sections.

A caboose rolls down the tracks to become a permanent part of the Depot, home of the Madison Senior Citizens. Under Beach and Recreation Department supervision until 1990, the group became the Madison Senior Citizens Council and later received full commission status. The facility is used evenings and weekends by other town organizations.

In June 1984, a new ambulance headquarters was dedicated to Legionnaires Peter Casula and Clayton Clark. Pete Casula (center) was the driver when town ambulance service was provided by the American Legion, Griswold Post. He was known to have made the Madison-New Haven Hospital run in 12 minutes flat.

Storefronts sometimes changed their names but the buildings in this section had remained the same for several decades. One long winter evening at the end of 1985, a fire started in a small convenience store basement and flowed through connected basements and up hollow interior walls to consume a major section of the stores shown above.

Fire companies from surrounding towns helped the Madison Fire Companies contain the fire to the buildings initially affected. Jolly's Drugstore was rebuilt, but Lupone's clothing store never reopened.

Halfway up the length of Madison, at the intersection of Durham Road and the Killingworth Turnpike, is the North Madison Circle. There, this group of buildings supplied North Madison with gasoline and with food until Robert's Food Center opened in 1983 a short distance to the east. The Circle Store, now a convenience store and deli (left), was originally situated in the small center building.

In 1981, the white two-story house on the far left and the three-story house on the far right were the only homes to be seen in this view looking across Fence Creek. This picture, taken in 1988, illustrates the new construction taking place all over Madison during the 1980s.

Ten

SHAPING THE FUTURE
1990–1998

The end of the 20th century finds Madison alive with diversity as its 16,400 citizens endeavor to shape the town's future. Controversy reflects what is still Madison's greatest asset—an active and involved population. Town boards and commissions remain largely volunteer.

The 1998 town budget of $11,900,000 and school budget of $25,400,000 were reviewed at public hearing with little dissension and easily passed in a budget referendum. A proposal to allow re-configuration of the Scranton parking lot also passed.

How many pictures have been taken from this spot! Since the advent of photography, this view of the downtown has reflected the evolving town, always representing the core of Madison. Completing the century's final decade, it seems appropriate to record the "now" as we note the changes over a hundred years and ponder those to come.

Memorials honoring Madisonians who gave their lives for their country grace the east end of the Green. The site of commemorative services on national holidays, the stones are revered as symbols of patriotism and sacrifice.

At one such service, on Memorial Day, 1992, Gordon King of the American Legion presented bound copies of the World War II newsletter, *News From Home*, to town organizations. Edited by Ward Scranton, the newsletters were filled with local news, gossip, and greetings to Americans at war, to whom they were treasured reminders of home.

High praise for training, efficiency, and unfailing dedication is but a limited expression of the gratitude owed the volunteer firemen of both Madison and North Madison. Their quick response to major alarms has contained many potentially disastrous fires, while relatively minor calls such as a car fire, being demonstrated here, are everyday work.

From one school nurse, the local Visiting Nurse Association has expanded into Community Care. The VNA of Madison's Strong House provides daily care and activities for senior citizens from both Madison and surrounding towns. Here, a bingo game is in progress under the supervision of Diane Cadwell, program assistant.

An old family business, the Munger Lumber Company long-served the construction needs of local builders. The business closed in 1996, after the death of Henry Munger, and the former lumberyard was soon replaced by newly constructed houses.

Summer visitors long constituted the town's major industry. Recently, a number of more conventional light industries have sprouted, to the benefit of the town. Garrity Industries, in addition to bringing its international markets and excellent reputation to Madison, also employs members of SARAH, Inc., to assemble flashlights.

Business and Legal Reports is another such welcomed addition to the town's economic life. BLR publishes reference books which explain government regulations to U.S. businesses. Employees package the reams of material that are shipped out daily.

When town government moved to the Hammonassett campus, Memorial Hall was rededicated and renovated for use as meeting rooms and the home of the Charlotte L. Evarts Memorial Archives. Tucked under scaffolding is the new elevator entrance that greatly increases accessibility to all three floors.

This impressive entrance to the new town office complex off Duck Hole Road features the town seal designed by Robert Terrill. The campus is also home to town athletic, educational, and recreational programs, as well as the offices of the Education Department.

This newly installed roadbed and track will soon carry the latest high-speed trains between New York and Boston. The juggernaut of progress has already claimed the old Horsepond Road bridge, seen here for the last time in 1998. Its replacement will connect realigned roads. Gone is the three-way roller coaster junction that was more effective in slowing traffic than any stoplight.

Once a community of westward bound pioneers, Genessee is now one of North Madison's newest housing developments. Priced around $370,000 for 3,400 square feet, this eight-room house reflects current design trends where kitchen and family room are each larger than the living room.

From one century to the next, the sea shapes the life of Madison. Shipping, fishing, summer residences, boating, and beaches, all have influenced its character. Farmlands grow houses; turnpikes replace trolleys; industries change. But inexorably, the sea, with its beauty and power, remains constant.

ACKNOWLEDGMENTS

It is with deep appreciation that we thank the following people for allowing us to use their photographs in this book: Mrs. Herbert T. Clark, George Doerrer, Joan Frye, George Gould, Joel Helander, Ray Hencir, Patricia Holdridge, Stuart Hotchkiss, Margaret Jennings, Dorothy Kelly, Carlene Kulisch of the South Central Regional Water Authority, Allin Miller, Dale Moore of The Source, Maria Elena Pignatelli, the E.C. Scranton Library, Jerome Wexler, True Wolff, Betty Pierce Wright, and Elizabeth Young of the *Shore Line Times*. By sharing their files, attics, and shoeboxes, they made this book possible.

Many others contributed information, research, and advice, and helped in other ways. Among those were John Atticks, Robert Brady of BLR, Ann Carlson of Garrity Industries, Fran Donnelly, Paul Edman, Nancy Farnan, Claire McKillip, Carol Speer, Marcia Stone, and Joanne Sullivan of the VNA of Madison. Special thanks to Shoreline Photographic Supply who somehow managed to get our photographs ready "yesterday."